M000028289

Shakespeare
Flush With Verse

Classic
Quotations
for Times of
Deep Thought

CIDER MILL
PRESS

BOOK
PUBLISHERS

Kennebunkport, Maine

SHAKESPEARE FLUSH WITH VERSE

13-Digit ISBN: 978-1-60433-139-4
10-Digit ISBN: 1-60433-139-9

This book may be ordered by mail from the publisher. Please
include $2.95 for postage and handling.
Please support your local bookseller first!

Books published by Cider Mill Press Book Publishers are
available at special discounts for bulk purchases in the United
States by corporations, institutions, and other organizations. For
more information, please contact the publisher.

Cider Mill Press Book Publishers
"Where good books are ready for press"
12 Port Farm Road
Kennebunkport, Maine 04046

Visit us on the web!
www.cidermillpress.com

Interior Design by Physioga
Printed in China

1 2 3 4 5 6 7 8 9 0
First Edition

Shakespeare
Flush With Verse

"Rough winds do shake the darling buds of May," wrote the great Bard. But maybe it was an inside joke!

Who knows what inspires great works of genius? Who knows when or where genius strikes——in bed? In a great library? In an outhouse?

Spending again what is already spent may have had a baser meaning.

William Shakespeare wrote on many subjects, including love, war, humor, and sex. Indeed, volumes have been written about the double meanings and sexual innuendos in his works. Not surprisingly, however, when one examines more closely [but not too closely], it's clear that he often made sport of our own personal lower depths. It seemed Shakespeare's subtext has escaped scholars worldwide...until now.

> "Diseased nature oftentimes breaks forth
> In strange eruptions."
> [KING HENRY IV, PART I; ACT III, SC. I]

Shakespeare was so right.

You'll feel right at home while reading this royally wonderful collection on a throne of your own. You'll be flush with laughter as your peruse these pages filled with Shakespeare's wit and wisdom, and you'll find hidden meanings in the Bard's writings you'd never known of before.

When King Lear bellowed at the raging storm, "Blow, winds, and crack your cheeks," we're almost sure he didn't intend to write those words on a men's-room stall for your amusement. That was our job. When Hamlet surmised, "Something is rotten in the state of Denmark," maybe he was referring to the royal bathroom.

Research has shown that indeed, the famed line from Macbeth screeched by the infamous three witches was actually an inside joke about the Globe's rather unworthy lavatory facilities:

"Fair is foul, and foul is fair:
Hover through the fog and filthy air."

This collection may be a little cheeky, but it's also a great relief. We've squeezed every line out of the Bard's plays to give you great satisfaction. Who knows what Shakespeare might have thought about, quill in hand, while sitting on his own royal throne in Stratford-on-Avon——the fair Rosamond? King Henry IV? Or last night's really tough mutton? Ugh!

Today Shakespeare is lauded and heralded as one of the greatest masters of the English language. But he was also a man with needs. And sometimes those needs were not to be filled, but rather to be emptied. Shakespeare is now fully exposed.

These are his departing thoughts!

Shakespeare Quotes

—

BOOK I

Shakespeare
Flush With Verse

1.
Asses are made to bear, and so are you.
THE TAMING OF THE SHREW, ACT II, SCENE I

2.
I like this place, and willingly would waste my time in it.
AS YOU LIKE IT, ACT II, SCENE IV

3.

All that follow their noses are led by their eyes but blind men; and there's not a nose among twenty but can smell him that's stinking.

KING LEAR, ACT II, SCENE IV

4.

All the world's a stage

AS YOU LIKE IT, ACT II, SCENE VII

5.

He hath eaten me out of house and home

KING HENRY IV, PART II, ACT II, SCENE I

6.

Why, I think so: I am not such an ass but I can keep my hand dry.

TWELFTH NIGHT, ACT I, SCENE III

7.

Something is rotten in the state of Denmark

HAMLET, ACT I, SCENE IV

8.
God and his angels
guard your
sacred throne
And make you long
become it!

HENRY V, ACT I, SCENE II

9.
I, having been
acquainted with the
smell before

TWO GENTLEMAN OF VERONA, ACT IV, SCENE IV

10.
Nothing in his life became him like the leaving it

MACBETH, ACT I, SCENE IV

11.
This royal throne of kings

KING RICHARD II, ACT II, SCENE I

12.

Be great in act, as
you have been in
thought.

THE LIFE AND DEATH OF KING JOHN,
ACT V, SCENE I

13.

Preposterous ass,
that never read so far
To know the cause
why music was
ordain'd!

TAMING OF THE SHREW, ACT III, SCENE I

14.

Every man has business and desire, Such as it is.

HAMLET, ACT I, SCENE V

15.

Praising what is lost makes the remembrance dear.

ALL'S WELL THAT ENDS WELL,
ACT V, SCENE III

16.
Make the coming
hour o'erflow
with joy,
And pleasure drown
the brim.

ALL'S WELL THAT ENDS WELL,
ACT II, SCENE IV

17.
Our bodies are
our gardens to
which our wills are
gardeners.

OTHELLO, ACT I, SCENE III

18.

Glory is like a
circle in the water,
Which never
ceaseth to
enlarge itself,
Till by
broad spreading it
disperses
to naught.

KING HENRY VI, PART I, ACT I, SCENE II

19.
Why, now blow
wind, swell billow,
and swim bark!
The storm is up, and
all is on the hazard.

JULIUS CAESAR, ACT V, SCENE I

20.
The rankest
compound of
villainous smell
that ever offended
nostrils.

THE MERRY WIVES OF WINDSOR,
ACT III, SCENE V

21.
A man of my kidney.
THE MERRY WIVES OF WINDSOR,
ACT III, SCENE V

22.
Whiles we are suitors to their throne, decays the thing we sue for
ANTONY AND CLEOPATRA, ACT II, SCENE I

23.
Comparisons are odorous.
MUCH ADO ABOUT NOTHING,
ACT III, SCENE V

24.
Sits the wind in that corner?

MUCH ADO ABOUT NOTHING,
ACT II, SCENE III

25.
Affliction may one day smile again; till then, sit thee down, sorrow.

LOVE'S LABOUR'S LOST, ACT I, SCENE I

26.

Bless thee, Bottom!
Bless thee! Thou art
translated.

A MIDSUMMER NIGHT'S DREAM,
ACT III, SCENE I

27.

Better three hours
too soon than a
minute too late.

THE MERRY WIVES OF WINDSOR,
ACT II, SCENE II

28.

Every one can
master a grief but he
that has it.

MUCH ADO ABOUT NOTHING,
ACT III, SCENE II

29.
It smells
to heaven.
HAMLET, ACT III, SCENE III

30.
Who riseth from
a feast
With that keen
appetite that he sits
down?
THE MERCHANT OF VENICE,
ACT II, SCENE VI

31.

The smell whereof shall breed a plague in France.

THE LIFE OF KING HENRY THE FIFTH,
ACT IV, SCENE III

32.

All the perfumes of Arabia will not sweeten this little hand.

MACBETH, ACT V, SCENE I

33.

This is a sorry sight.

MACBETH, ACT II, SCENE II

34.

I do repent; but heaven hath pleas'd it so to punish me with this

HAMLET, ACT III, SCENE IV

35.

Thus bad begins and worse remains behind.

HAMLET, ACT III, SCENE IV

36.

Every inch a king!

KING LEAR, ACT IV, SCENE VI

37.
With this special observance, that you o'erstep not the modesty of nature

HAMLET, ACT III, SCENE II

38.
O, my offence is rank it smells to heaven

HAMLET, ACT III, SCENE III

39.
A good riddance.

TROILUS AND CRESSIDA, ACT II, SCENE I

40.

See, how she leans
her cheek upon
her hand!
O that I were a glove
upon that hand, that
I might touch that
cheek!

ROMEO AND JULIET, ACT II, SCENE II

41.

Delays have
dangerous ends.

KING HENRY THE SIXTH, PART I,
ACT III, SCENE II

42.

Thou losest thy old smell.

AS YOU LIKE IT, ACT I, SCENE II

43.

Fair is foul, and foul is fair.

MACBETH, ACT I, SCENE I

44.

A very ancient and fish-like smell.

THE TEMPEST, ACT II, SCENE II

45.

One touch of nature
makes the whole
world kin.

TROILUS AND CRESSIDA,
ACT III, SCENE III

46.

You are an
alchemist; make
gold of that.

THE LIFE OF TIMON OF ATHENS,
ACT V, SCENE I

47.

Now good digestion
wait on appetite,
And health on both!

MACBETH, ACT III, SCENE IV

48.
Must I hold a candle to my shames?

THE MERCHANT OF VENICE,
ACT II, SCENE VI

49.
Double, double toil and trouble; Fire burn, and cauldron bubble.

MACBETH, ACT IV, SCENE I

50.

I must have liberty
Withal, as large a
charter as the wind,
To blow on whom I
please.

AS YOU LIKE IT, ACT II, SCENE VII

51.

Can one desire too
much of a good
thing?

AS YOU LIKE IT, ACT IV, SCENE I

52.

Make the coming
hour o'erflow
with joy,
And pleasure drown
the brim.

ALL 'S WELL THAT ENDS WELL,
ACT II, SCENE IV

53.

He does it with a
better grace, but I do
it more natural.

TWELFTH NIGHT, ACT II, SCENE III

54.
The ripest fruit first falls.

KING RICHARD II, ACT II, SCENE I

55.
Go thrust him out at gates, and let him smell
His way to Dover.

KING LEAR, ACT III, SCENE VII

56.
Diseased Nature oftentimes breaks forth
In strange eruptions.

KING HENRY IV, PART I, ACT III, SCENE I

57.
A thing devised by the enemy.

KING RICHARD III, ACT V, SCENE III

58.
He was a man Of an unbounded stomach.

KING HENRY VIII, ACT IV, SCENE II

59.
A load would sink a navy.

KING HENRY VIII, ACT III, SCENE II

60.
Thou hast done a deed whereat valour will weep.

CORIOLANUS, ACT V, SCENE VI

61.

The heaven's breath
Smells wooingly
here: no jutty, frieze,
Buttress, nor coign
of vantage,
but this bird
Hath made his
pendent bed and
procreant cradle:
Where they most
breed and haunt, I
have observed,
The air is delicate.

MACBETH, ACT I, SCENE VI

62.

Truth is truth
To the end of
reckoning.

MEASURE FOR MEASURE, ACT V, SCENE I

63.

Stoop, boys.
This gate
Instructs you how
t' adore the heavens
and bows you
To a morning's holy
office.

CYMBELINE, ACT III, SCENE III

64.

She swore, i' faith,
'twas strange, 'twas
passing strange;
'Twas pitiful, 'twas
wondrous pitiful.

OTHELLO, ACT I, SCENE III

65.

All that glisters is not
gold; Often have you
heard that told; Many
a man his life hath
sold; But my outside
to behold.

THE MERCHANT OF VENICE,
ACT II, SCENE VII

66.

O, it came o'er
my ear like the
sweet sound
That breathes
upon a bank
of violets,
Stealing and
giving odor.

TWELFTH NIGHT, ACT I, SCENE I

67.
O villainy! Ho! Let the door be lock'd. Treachery! Seek it out.

HAMLET, ACT V, SCENE II

68.
Hoy-day! What a sweep of vanity comes this way!

THE LIFE OF TIMON OF ATHENS, ACT I, SCENE II

69.

In nature
there's no
blemish but the
mind;
None can be
called deformed
but the unkind.

TWELFTH NIGHT, ACT III, SCENE IV

70.

I must to the barber's, monsieur; for me thinks I am marvellous hairy about the face; and I am such a tender ass, if my hair do but tickle me, I must scratch.

MIDSUMMER NIGHT'S DREAM,
ACT IV, SCENE I

71.

The houses he makes last till doomsday.

HAMLET PRINCE OF DENMARK,
ACT V, SCENE I

72.
Untimely storms makes men expect a dearth.

THE TRAGEDY OF KING RICHARD THE
THIRD, ACT II, SCENE III

73.
Blow, winds, and crack your cheeks.

KING LEAR, ACT III, SCENE II

74.

A little gale will soon
disperse that cloud
And blow it to
the source from
whence it came

KING HENRY THE SIXTH, PART III,
ACT V, SCENE III

75.

Yet who would have
thought the old man
to have had so much
blood in him?

MACBETH, ACT V, SCENE I

76.

Come, you virtuous
ass, you bashful fool,
must you be blushing?

HENRY IV, ACT II, SCENE I

77.

Let me wipe it first; it
smells of mortality.

KING LEAR ACT IV, SCENE VI

78.

What's the business,
That such a hideous
trumpet calls to parley
The sleepers of the
house? Speak, speak!

MACBETH, ACT II, SCENE III

79.
The empty vessel makes the greatest sound.

THE LIFE OF KING HENRY THE FIFTH,
ACT IV, SCENE V

80.
It appeareth nothing to me but a foul and pestilent congregation of vapors.

HAMLET, ACT II, SCENE II

81.

The barge
she sat in,
like a burnished
throne,
Burned on the
water: the poop
was beaten gold;
Purple the sails,
and
so perfumed that
The winds were
lovesick with
them.

ANTONY AND CLEOPATRA, ACT II, SCENE II

82.

I will be correspondent to command,
And do my spiriting gently.

THE TEMPEST, ACT I, SCENE II

83.

Deeper than e'er plummet sounded.

THE TEMPEST, ACT III, SCENE III

84.

With the most noble bottom of our fleet,

TWELFTH NIGHT, ACT V, SCENE I

Excellent!
I smell a device.

TITUS ANDRONICUS, ACT II, SCEN

86.
His nature is too
noble for the worl
He would not flatte
Neptune for his
trident,
Or Jove for's power t
thunder.

CORIOLANUS, ACT III, SCENE I

87.
The true beginning
of our end.

A MIDSUMMER NIGHT'

88.

My ventures are not in one bottom trusted,
Nor to one place.

THE MERCHANT OF VENICE, ACT I, SCENE I

89.

I have seen the day of wrong through the little hole of discretion.

LOVE'S LABOUR'S LOST, ACT V, SCENE II

91.

Thou know'st, the
first time that we
smell the air
We wawl and cry.

KING LEAR, ACT IV, SCENE VI

92.

Thou took'st a begg
wouldst have mad
my throne

93.
For it so falls out
That what we have
we prize not to the
worth.

MUCH ADO ABOUT NOTHING,
ACT IV, SCENE I

94.
Forsake thy seat,
I do beseech thee,
captain,
And hear me speak
a word.

ANTONY AND CLEOPATRA, ACT II, SCENE VII

95.

Pleasure and action
make the hours
seem short.

OTHELLO, ACT II, SCENE III

96.

A goodly house: the
feast smells well;
but I
Appear not like a
guest.

CORIOLANUS, ACT IV, SCENE V

97.

Into thin air

THE TEMPEST, ACT IV, SCENE I

98.

That this foul deed
shall smell above
the earth
With carrion men,
groaning for burial.

JULIUS CEASAR, ACT III, SCENE I

99.

O, what men dare do!
What men may do!
What men daily do,
not knowing what
they do!

MUCH ADO ABOUT NOTHING, ACT IV, SCENE I

100.
What's done is done.
MACBETH, ACT III, SCENE II

101.
Out, damned spot!
Out, I say!
MACBETH, ACT V, SCENE I

102.
This castle hath a pleasant seat; the air Nimbly and sweetly recommends itself Unto our gentle senses.
MACBETH, ACT I, SCENE VI

103.

By the pricking of
my thumbs,
Something wicked
this way comes.
Open, locks,
Whoever knocks!

MACBETH ACT IV, SCENE I

104.

Indeed, it does stink
in some sort, sir; but
yet, sir, I would prove

MEASURE FOR MEASURE, ACT III, SCENE II

105.

Some rise by sin, and
some by virtue fall

MEASURE FOR MEASURE, ACT II, SCENE I

106.

O noble strain!

CYMBELINE, ACT IV, SCENE II

107.

Ay, 'twas he that told
me first:
An honest man he is,
and hates the slime
That sticks on filthy
deeds.

OTHELLO, ACT V, SCENE II

108.

Believe me, no: I
thank my fortune
for it,
My ventures are
not in one bottom
trusted,
Nor to one place;
nor is my whole
estate
Upon the fortune of
this present year:
Therefore my
merchandise makes
me not sad.

ANTONIO AND CLEOPATRA, ACT I, SCENE I

109.

In nature is a
tyranny; it hath bee
The untimely
emptying of the
happy throne
And fall of many
kings.

MACBETH, ACT IV, SCENE III

110.

I am stuffed, cousi
I cannot smell.

MUCH ADO ABOUT NOTHING,
ACT III, SCENE IV

III.

His left cheek is a cheek of two pile and a half, but his right cheek is worn bare.

ALL'S WELL THAT ENDS WELL,
ACT IV, SCENE V

112.

Do thou amend thy face, and I'll amend my life: thou art our admiral, thou bearest the lantern in the poop, but 'tis in the nose of thee; thou art the Knight of the Burning Lamp.

HENRY IV, ACT III, SCENE III

113.

Thou art sensible in nothing but blows, and so is an ass.

COMEDY OF ERRORS, ACT III, SCENE II

114.

Then hear me, gracious sovereign, and you peers, That owe yourselves, your lives and services To this imperial throne

HENRY V, ACT I, SCENE II

115.
O this woodcock, what an ass it is!
TAMING OF THE SHREW, ACT I, SCENE II

116.
Who ever yet could sound thy bottom?
CYMBELINE, ACT IV, SCENE II

117.

For I am stifled with this smell of sin.

JULIUS CAESAR, ACT III, SCENE I

118.

Out of our question wipe him.

ANTONY AND CLEOPATRA, ACT II, SCENE II

119.

Here is my throne, bid kings come bow to it.

KING JOHN, ACT III, SCENE I

120.

Whereto we see in all things nature tends——Foh! one may smell in such a will most rank

OTHELLO, ACT III, SCENE III

121.
But with his last attempt he wiped it out;
CORIOLANUS, ACT V, SCENE III

122.
My words fly up, my thoughts remain below
HAMLET, ACT III, SCENE III

123.
Let me wipe off this honourable dew
HENRY VI, ACT II, SCENE V

124.
The winds grow high; so do your stomachs, lords.

HENRY VI, ACT II, SCENE I

125.
What an ass it is!

CORIOLANUS, ACT IV, SCENE V

ABOUT CIDER MILL PRESS BOOK PUBLISHERS

GOOD IDEAS ripen with time. From seed to harvest, Cider Mill Press brings fine reading, information, and entertainment together between the covers of its creatively crafted books. Our Cider Mill bears fruit twice a year, publishing a new crop of titles each Spring and Fall.

Visit us on the web at
www.cidermillpress.com
or write to us at
12 Port Farm Road
Kennebunkport, Maine 04046

CIDER MILL
PRESS

BOOK
PUBLISHERS